Hours of fun and ghoulish laughter with ...

SPOOKY WORD PLAY

beaver books

Publishing Director: Erika Szucs
Writer: Diandra D'Alessio   Editors: Diandra D'Alessio, Clarissa Sorgiovanni
Cover Design: Ella Fert   Page Design: Robert Nikolakakis   Illustrator: Mike Polito

Funded by the Government of Canada | Canadä

INSTRUCTIONS:

Wordplay is the silliest, funniest, happiest, coolest, most awesome word game you'll ever play.

Just follow these simple directions:

Before every story in this book, you'll find four columns of words, each marked with a symbol. Each symbol represents the following:

Symbols

NOUN

VERB

ADJECTIVE

WACKY WORDS

In each story, you'll find blank spaces marked with any one of the symbols above. Fill in each blank space with a word from that column until all the blank spaces in the story are filled. Finally, read your Wordplay aloud to see what kind of wacky, silly, hilarious story you've created.

Change the words, and you'll have a different story every time!

SPOOKY WORD PLAY

REVIEW

A NOUN  is the name of a person, place, or thing. *Teacher, park, ear,* and *bus* are **nouns.**

A VERB  is an action word. *Fly, run, throw,* and *jump* are **verbs.**

An ADJECTIVE  describes something or somebody. *Sweet, cool, awesome, serious,* and *funny* are **adjectives.**

A WACKY WORD  is any word that will make the story wackier.

WORD PLAY
SPOOKY

Trick or Treat!

Complete the story using the word bank on this page—
or use your own words!

NOUNS

Astronaut
Butterfly
Cat
Dragon
Knight
Mummy
Pumpkin
Scarecrow
Superhero
Vampire
Witch
Zombie

ADJECTIVES

Big
Chewy
Crunchy
Delicious
Full
Funny
Heavy
Purple
Scary
Sparkly
Spooky
Sweet

VERBS

Break
Chew
Crunch
Devour
Eat
Explode
Have
Jump
Relax
Sink
Squash
Wait

WACKY WORDS

Bloop
Caboodle
Huzzah
Jujube
Kooky
Razzmatazz
Squeegee
Whatzit
Whoop
Wonky
Zonk
Zoodle

Trick or Treat

My friends and I had so much fun trick-or-treating last night!

I dressed up as a/an _____ , Mia dressed up as a/an
                        N

_____ _____ , and Noah dressed up as
         W   N

a/an _____ _____ . We passed by many
          A   N

_____ houses and got lots of _____
         A   A

candy. My favorite is the _____ bar. I can
                                 W

_____ five of them in one sitting! Mia's favorite candy
         V

is the sour _____ , while Noah likes _____
                  W   A

chocolate. By the end of the night, our buckets were so

_____ , we thought they would _____ !
         A   V

I can't _____ for next Halloween!
              V

SPOOKY WORD PLAY

A Scary Movie

Complete the story using the word bank on this page—
or use your own words!

NOUNS

Bucket
Chair
Couch
Creature
Ghoul
Phantom
Room
Seat
Spirit
Street
Tree
Window

ADJECTIVES

Awesome
Cool
Dark
Friendly
Funny
Happy
Quiet
Scared
Shocked
Spooky
Stormy
Weird

VERBS

Call
Find
Hear
Hunt
Laugh
Nap
See
Sleep
Smell
Sneeze
Speak
Yodel

WACKY WORDS

Boo
Flimflam
Gadzooks
Gaga
Huzzah
Kazoo
Kerfuffle
Schmooze
Teehee
Willy-nilly
Yahoo
Yippee

A Scary Movie

My family and I watched a horror movie called " _____

A (noun/ghost)

_____ ." It stars my favorite actors, Jason

N (noun/bat)

_____ and Ashley _____ . They play a/an

W (word/pumpkin)   **N** (noun/bat)

_____ couple who like to _____ ghosts!

A (noun/ghost)   **V** (verb/spider)

One scene was so _____ , it had me on the edge of my

A (noun/ghost)

_____ . The couple use a _____ board to

N (noun/bat)   **W** (word/pumpkin)

try to _____ a ghost, when suddenly, they hear

V (verb/spider)

" _____ !" I was so _____ that I couldn't

W (word/pumpkin)   **A** (noun/ghost)

_____ ! I was afraid to _____ that night,

V (verb/spider)   **V** (verb/spider)

but my mom said there's no such thing as ghosts. Then why

did I hear " _____ " outside my _____ ?

W (word/pumpkin)   **N** (noun/bat)

SPOOKY WORDPLAY

My Halloween Costume

Complete the story using the word bank on this page—
or use your own words!

NOUNS

Alien
Angel
Belt
Bumblebee
Butterfly
Doctor
Hat
Pilot
Scarecrow(s)
Scarf
Vampire
Zombie

ADJECTIVES

Amazing
Awesome
Beautiful
Big
Cool
Fancy
Fluffy
Gold
Neon
Scary
Shiny
Studded

VERBS

Adore
Dance
Decorate
Find
Giggle
Laugh
Love
Paint
See
Show
Wear
Win

WACKY WORDS

Awooga
Bauble
Brouhaha
Fizzy
Kaboom
Malarkey
Phooey
Pogo
Slinky
Spiffy
Woot
Zigzag

My Halloween Costume

I _____ my _____ Halloween costume!
     (verb)   (adjective)

This year, I'm going as a/an _____ _____
                                  (word)   (noun)

noun. I borrowed a/an _____ _____ from
                          (adjective)   (noun)

my mom, a/an _____ shirt from my sister, a pair
                 (word)

of _____ pants from my dad, and my brother's
       (adjective)

_____ shoes. I'll also _____ my face with
    (adjective)   (verb)

_____ makeup. My favorite part of my costume, though,
    (adjective)

is the _____ necklace. When I _____ it, I feel
           (adjective)   (verb)

_____ ! I can't wait to _____ my friends and
    (adjective)   (verb)

hear them go "_____ !" Today's the _____
                   (word)   (adjective)

costume contest at school. I hope I _____ !
                                         (verb)

WORD PLAY
SPOOKY

Halloween Party

Complete the story using the word bank on this page—
or use your own words!

NOUNS

Apple(s)
Candy(ies)
Chocolate(s)
Corn
Ghost(s)
Gumdrop(s)
Licorice
Lollipop(s)
Marshmallow(s)
Pecan(s)
Pumpkin(s)
Scarecrow

ADJECTIVES

Big
Eager
Excited
Fresh
Funny
Happy
Huge
Scary
Silly
Sour
Spooky
Sweet

VERBS

Bringing
Carving
Dancing
Decorating
Eating
Laughing
Painting
Sharing
Singing
Smiling
Swapping
Telling

WACKY WORDS

Baa-baa
Boggle
Claptrap
Cubby
Egads
Hijinks
Hullaballoo
Jabber
Nifty
Snoot
Spork
Whoop

Halloween Party

My friends and I are _____ (A) for the Halloween party!

We're all dressed up and each of us is _____ (V)

something. I'm bringing my mom's famous _____ (W)

cookies, Sophia is bringing candy _____ (N) , and Lucas is

bringing _____ (N) pie. The party will be at my friend

Elijah's house on _____ (W) Street. You can tell it's his house

because there's a/an _____ (A) _____ (N) on the

front lawn. We'll be _____ (V) along to _____ (A)

music, _____ (V) pumpkins, and _____ (V)

_____ (A) stories! Elijah will also give us loot bags full of

_____ (A) _____ (N) . He throws the best parties!

WORD PLAY (SPOOKY)

The Ghost

Complete the story using the word bank on this page— or use your own words!

NOUNS

Bathroom
Bedroom
Den
Dining room
Family
Friends
Hallway
Kitchen
Parents
Sisters
Brothers
Study

ADJECTIVES

Amazing
Billowy
Cool
Eerie
Funny
Light
Pretty
Scary
Spooky
Unusual
Weird
White

VERBS

Cooking
Dancing
Eating
Floating
Flying
Jumping
Laughing
Reading
Running
Screaming
Singing
Skipping

WACKY WORDS

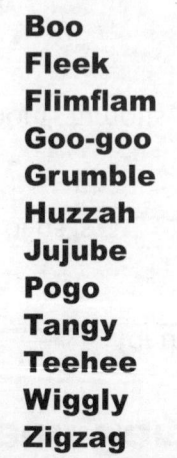

Boo
Fleek
Flimflam
Goo-goo
Grumble
Huzzah
Jujube
Pogo
Tangy
Teehee
Wiggly
Zigzag

The Ghost

Last night, I thought I saw a ghost! I was _____ (V) in

the _____ (N) when I suddenly heard a loud

"_____ (W)!" It was so _____ (A)! I then saw this

_____ (A) figure wearing a/an _____ (A) sheet.

It seemed to be _____ (V) in the air! "_____ (W)!"

I said, _____ (V) out of the room. How would I tell my

_____ (N) that there was a ghost in the house? They

heard my _____ (V) and came downstairs. "That's no

ghost!" they said. "It's just _____ (W) in a blanket!" That's

right—the ghost was my dog all along!

Witches' Brew

Complete the recipe using the word bank on this page—
or use your own words!

NOUNS

Apple(s)
Cinnamon
Eel(s)
Frog(s)
Newt(s)
Nutmeg
Plum(s)
Pumpkin(s)
Salt
Spider(s)
Sugar
Yam(s)

ADJECTIVES

Big
Black
Blue
Chilled
Cold
Electric
Fresh
Frozen
Golden
Old
Purple
White

VERBS

Blend
Combine
Dance
Giggle
Jump
Mix
Puree
Simmer
Sing
Somersault
Stir
Talk

WACKY WORDS

Awooga
Bock-bock
Brouhaha
Frizzle
Hullaballoo
Jamboree
Kerplunk
Lollygag
Loop-de-loop
Razzle-dazzle
Whoop-de-doo
Zoom-zoom

Witches' Brew

Ingredients:

1 eye of _____
(N — bat)

3 _____ _____
(A — ghost) *(N — bat)*

A pinch of _____
(N — bat)

_____ juice
(W — pumpkin)

Directions:

_____ all ingredients into a/an
(V — spider)

_____ cauldron.
(A — ghost)

_____ until the drink is warm, but not boiling.
(V — spider)

Serve _____ in _____ glasses.
(A — ghost) *(W — pumpkin)*

Pumpkin Decorating

Complete the story using the word bank on this page—
or use your own words!

NOUNS

Buttons
Candy(ies)
Chocolate(s)
Family
Feathers
Glitter
Leaves
Licorice
Paint(s)
Ribbon(s)
Siblings
Stickers

ADJECTIVES

Awesome
Big
Bright
Cool
Fun
Nice
Old
Shiny
Silly
Small
Sparkly
Young

VERBS

Carve
Dance
Decorate
Hold
Jump
Laugh
Put
Run
Smile
Stick
Wash
Yodel

WACKY WORDS

Bloop
Bobble
Doozy
Gadzooks
Kerfuffle
Kooky
Loofah
Phooey
Shazam
Snazzy
Splat
Willy-nilly

Pumpkin Decorating

After a/an _____ trip to the farm, my _____

and I are ready to decorate our pumpkins! We're too _____

to _____ them ourselves, so my parents will help

us. After the pumpkins are carved, we get to _____

all sorts of _____ things on them. I like _____

_____ and _____ _____ ,

while my sister likes _____ tape. My brother usually puts

_____ and _____ _____

to make a/an _____ smile. Of course, no pumpkin

is complete without a good _____ . When we put them

on the front porch, they'll surely make people _____ !

Apple Bobbing

Complete the story using the word bank on this page—
or use your own words!

NOUNS

Back
Bucket
Container
Ear(s)
Hat
Head
Leg(s)
Mouth
Toe(s)
Tub
Vat
Water

ADJECTIVES

Cold
Cool
Dense
Exciting
Fun
Funny
Groovy
Interesting
Large
Round
Shiny
Sweet

VERBS

Bend
Catch
Dance
Fill
Float
Grab
Hold
Jump
Kneel
Laugh
Show
Tell

WACKY WORDS

Baa-baa
Burpee
Caboodle
Fizzy
Gizmo
Jujube
Kazoo
Loosey-goosey
Whatzit
Wonky
Yoink
Yowza

Apple Bobbing

Have you ever tried apple bobbing? It's so _____ !
A

Let me _____ you how to play. First, find
V

a/an _____ _____ . _____
A   N   V

it with _____ water, and make sure it's not too
W

_____ . Next, add about a dozen _____
A   W

apples. Apples are less _____ than water, so they'll
A

_____ in the _____ . To start playing,
V   N

_____ in front of the tub, hands behind your
V

_____ . Lower your head into the water and try to
N

_____ an apple with your teeth. The first person to
V

_____ an apple in their _____ wins!
V   N

SPOOKY WORD PLAY

The Haunted House

Complete the story using the word bank on this page—
or use your own words!

NOUNS

Arm(s)
Candle(s)
Cobwebs
Eye(s)
Floor(s)
House
Light(s)
Mansion
Mirror(s)
Room(s)
Statue(s)

ADJECTIVES

Blurry
Creaky
Eerie
Funny
Happy
Loud
Mysterious
Pretty
Spooky
Squeaky
Stormy
Weird

VERBS

Bolted
Cartwheeled
Hopped
Jogged
Ran
Sang
Somersaulted
Stepped
Walked
Went
Yodeled
Zigzagged

WACKY WORDS

Awooga
Bloop
Bock-bock
Boo
Derp
Froufrou
Gadzooks
Huzzah
Jinx
Yeet
Yippee
Yoo-hoo

The Haunted House

It was a dark and _____ (A) night when we went to the

haunted house. As soon as we _____ (V) in, we heard

_____ (A) " _____ (W) !" and " _____ (W) !"

noises. There were _____ (A) _____ (N)

everywhere and the _____ (N) was _____ (A)

when we _____ (V) on it. Still, we wanted to see more.

We _____ (V) upstairs and saw a/an _____ (W)

painting. It was very _____ (A) , so we _____ (V)

to it to get a closer look. Suddenly, its _____ (N) were

moving! We were so scared we _____ (V) out of the

_____ (N) . Strangely enough, I want to go again!

SPOOKY WORD PLAY

The UFO Sighting

Complete the story using the word bank on this page—
or use your own words!

NOUNS

Antenna(s)
Cat(s)
Dog(s)
Family
Friend(s)
Gift(s)
Giggle(s)
Nose(s)
Sibling(s)
Skin
Smile(s)
Wave(s)

ADJECTIVES

Amazing
Awesome
Bright
Brown
Huge
Little
Mysterious
Purple
Puzzled
Shiny
Sleepy
Worried

VERBS

Answered
Appeared
Disappeared
Exclaimed
Flew
Landed
Looked
Pointed
Sang
Shouted
Spoke
Whispered

WACKY WORDS

Ahoy-hoy
Aye-aye
Ballyhoo
Dabba
Egad
Kaput
Pogo
Quack
Shazam
Shoop
Yippee
Zoom

The UFO Sighting

Last night, my _____ and I saw a/an _____
(N) (A)

object in the sky. " _____ ! It's a spaceship!"
(W)

I _____ . It came closer and let out a beam of
(V)

_____ light. Suddenly, two aliens _____ .
(A) (V)

They had green _____ , _____ eyes,
(N) (A)

and _____ a/an _____ language.
(V) (A)

" _____ !" one said to the other. " _____ !"
(W) (W)

the other _____ . Then, one _____ at us and
(V) (V)

said, " _____ !" We were a bit _____ , until the
(W) (A)

other alien _____ at us and gave us a nice _____ .
(V) (N)

They _____ into the night, like a shooting star!
(V)

The Monster

Complete the story using the word bank on this page—
or use your own words!

NOUNS

Antenna(s)
Arm(s)
Bow(s)
Buddy(ies)
Ear(s)
Eye(s)
Friend(s)
Hand(s)
Horn(s)
Leg(s)
Toe(s)
Tusk(s)

ADJECTIVES

Big
Bright
Fluffy
Friendly
Glowing
Green
Happy
Long
Orange
Secret
Scary
Shiny

VERBS

Bake
Create
Dance
Describe
Eat
Explore
Laugh
Listen
Make
Play
See
Sing

WACKY WORDS

Caboodle
Diddly
Gaggle
Gizmo
Grumble
Jujube
Phooey
Razzle-dazzle
Scribble
Slinky
Spork
Yowza

The Monster

If you were to _____ a monster, what would it be like? My
(V)

monster is named _____ . It has three _____
(W)   (A)

_____ , two _____ _____ , and
(N)   (A)   (N)

_____ fur. It also has two _____ on its head.
(A)   (N)

It likes to _____ sandwiches made of _____ ,
(V)   (W)

_____ to _____ music, and play
(V)   (A)

_____ -ball. Some monsters are _____ , but
(W)   (A)

not mine! It's very _____ and gives _____
(A)   (A)

hugs. We like to _____ together and we have our own
(V)

_____ language called _____ . It may be
(A)   (W)

a monster, but it's my best _____ too!
(N)

SPOOKY WORD PLAY

The Werewolf

Complete the story using the word bank on this page—
or use your own words!

NOUNS

Cabin
Eye(s)
Fur
Hoodie
Howl
Jeans
Moon
Pants
Shirt
Tent
Whoop
Yodel

ADJECTIVES

Amazing
Awesome
Big
Blue
Brown
Fearsome
Full
Loud
Quiet
Sharp
Sparkly
Yellow

VERBS

Bolted
Bounced
Cartwheeled
Danced
Hopped
Ran
Saw
Skipped
Spotted
Turned
Vanished
Walked

WACKY WORDS

Aha
Bock-bock
Boo
Fleek
Huzzah
Kumquat
Lala
Oopsie
Umpteen
Whatzit
Wonky
Yippee

The Werewolf

One time, I dreamed I _____ a werewolf! He was
(V)

half-human, half-_____ , with brown _____
(W) *(N)*

and _____ teeth. He _____ on two legs
(A) *(V)*

and wore _____ _____ and a checkered
(A) *(N)*

_____ . He howled at the _____ moon
(N) *(A)*

and _____ into the woods. I followed him and then
(V)

heard a/an _____ _____ . Just like that, he
(A) *(N)*

_____ , but I then saw a man wearing the same clothes!
(V)

Before I could say _____ , he _____ into
(W) *(V)*

a/an _____ , and I woke up. I guess I'll have to wait
(N)

until the next full _____ !
(N)

Song of the Witches

Complete the story using the word bank on this page—
or use your own words!

NOUNS N

Bat
Cauldron
Crow
Ear
Eye
Fang
Heart
Llama
Moth
Sheep
Tail
Tongue

ADJECTIVES A

Bright
Deep
Electric
Fluffy
Funny
Gooey
Kooky
Pretty
Purple
Quiet
Sweet
Well

VERBS V

Boil
Bubble
Burn
Cook
Crackle
Hiss
Jump
Roast
Sing
Sizzle
Squeak
Toil

WACKY WORDS W

Bungee
Claptrap
Fluffernutter
Jamboree
Kaput
Nifty
Quibble
Snazzy
Topsy-turvy
Tweet
Yuzu
Zoot

Song of the Witches

Double, double _____ and trouble, fire

_____ and cauldron bubble. _____

of a _____ snake, in the cauldron boil and bake.

Eye of newt and toe of frog, wool of _____

and _____ of dog. _____ 's fork

and _____ -worm's sting, lizard's leg and
.

_____ 's wing. For a charm of _____

trouble, like a _____ boil and bubble. Double,

double _____ and trouble, fire burn and cauldron

_____ . Cool it with a baboon's _____ ,

then the charm is _____ and good.

The Corn Maze

Complete the story using the word bank on this page—
or use your own words!

NOUNS

Chicken(s)
Clown(s)
House
Monster(s)
Night
Scarecrow(s)
School
Skeleton(s)
Spiderweb(s)
Street
Week
Zombie(s)

ADJECTIVES

Amazing
Awesome
Cool
Funny
Ginormous
Great
Huge
Pretty
Scary
Sparkly
Spooky
Tiny

VERBS

Adore
Dance
Exit
Find
Hop
Jump
Leave
Love
Scream
Solve
Walk
Whisper

WACKY WORDS

Awooga
Bleurgh
Boo
Eek
Flimflam
Kazoo
Pizazz
Quack-quack
Slurp
Tippytoe
Whoopsie
Zoom

The Corn Maze

I _____ corn mazes! There's this _____
(V)   (A)

one near my _____ . I went with my friends last
(N)

_____ and we had a/an _____ time. We
(N)   (A)

had to _____ our way through the maze while also
(V)

dealing with _____ characters, _____ ends,
(A)   (A)

and creepy _____ . There was also _____
(N)   (W)

music playing that made us _____ . One guy dressed
(V)

as a _____ was so _____ , we said
(N)   (A)

" _____ !" and ran away as fast as we could. I was
(W)

_____ that we wouldn't _____ the maze,
(A)   (V)

but we saw a/an _____ sign saying that we made it. Phew!
(A)

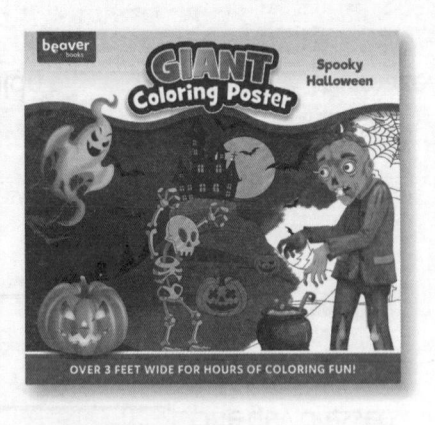

Visit our website to find more quality products:

www.pappinternational.com